The She-Preneur Journey:

The 10 Indepensable Things Every

Woman Must Do

on the

Pathway to Success

Luberta Lytle

Rhonda McAlister

Rhonda's Dedication:

I dedicate this book to every single mom who has a dream to become an entrepreneur and recognizes the sacrifices that will have to be made and seeks out to make her visualization a realization.

Luberta's Dedication:

I dedicate this book to every female who has been told that they are not enough but instead of playing the victim role they have decided to become victorious by walking in their divine purpose and start living the life they so desire the live.

You must not rely on the information in the e-book as an alternative to [legal / medical / financial / taxation / accountancy advice from an appropriately qualified professional. If you have any specific questions about any [legal / medical / financial / taxation / accountancy matter you should consult an appropriately qualified professional.

Enforcement of copyright

We take the protection of our copyright very seriously.

www.seqlegal.com

Table of Contents

Purpose Driven

Luberta's Story

We all have a story to share, but the question is, are you willing to tell you story? I am saying, yes and here it is.

I had my first child at the age of fourteen. I became pregnant again at the age of sixteen. Two children and two different fathers, by the age of sixteen. This time should have been happy and exciting, but instead I had to grow up and become someone's mother. I did finish high school, despite of adults and classmates telling me that I would not graduate. Was is hard having two toddlers and completing school? Yes, but I figured society had already labeled me as a teenage mom and I didn't want the labeled high school dropout too.

I had my third child at the age of twenty. My middle and youngest children have the same father. Still unmarried and now with three children. Finally, I decided that I needed to make some changes in my life. First off, I decided that I didn't want any more children. I spoke with my gynecologist regarding measures that I could take to ensure that I wouldn't get pregnant again. He was very reluctant to discuss this matter, but then I convinced him that something needed to be done. After debating with him over several months, we decided it would benefit me to have a surgical procedure called tubal ligation performed after the delivery of my last child. I had produced three children and

5

had no desire to produce any more. Shortly after turning twenty-one, I had the surgery. In addition to all of this, I decided I needed to find a job to take care of my children, instead of relying on the monthly welfare check. Don't get me wrong it served its purpose and provided me with some type of income to take care of my kids, but I desired more for me and my kids. Ironically my check still came from the state, but at least this time it came twice a month instead of monthly. I felt good about being able to take care of my children.

Then tragedy struck. My mother got sick shortly after I received my new job. She was diagnosed with breast cancer and passed away before, I reached my one-year anniversary with working for the state. At the age of twenty-one, I lost my mom. I felt so lost without her, but at least she knew that me and my kids would be okay. I got married shortly after my mother passed away and this lasted for only three years.

Then yet again life reared its ugly head and at the age of twenty-nine, had my own scare with cancer. I received the news from my gynecologist that I had precancerous cells located in my cervix and needed surgery to correct the problem. Surgery turned into a hysterectomy to correct the problem. Guess that meant that I would not have any more children.

Soon enough my children would bless me with grandchildren. My middle son gave me two grandchildren in one year and my baby girl, gave me one grandbaby in the same year. I never thought that I would be a grandmother at the age of thirty-five. I presume if you have your kids at early, then you become a grandmother early.

My life changed at the age of forty. I became a grandmother/mom to my granddaughter. She was only two, when she moved into my house. I had forgot what it was like to raise a toddler. I truly gave much respect to all the single mothers during this time. I had my life all planned, but sometimes things don't go as planned, but we adjusted. I decided to give marriage another try too. Now, I have more grandchildren too. My oldest son has blessed me with two children with his wife. My middle son, has given me one more grandbaby and my daughter has added to the collection too, she has given me four more grandchildren. Guess, that gives me a grand total of eleven grandbabies. All, I can say is wow at this point in time.

My life has had many ups and downs, but through it all I knew that there was still so much more that I needed to do. I returned to school at the age of forty-five. I felt good about obtaining more education, but still felt like it was still something missing. I received my Bachelor's degree, but still felt a void in my life. I returned to school and obtained my Master's degree, but still felt this void in my life. I am truly blessed to have the degrees, but still searched for more out of my life. I finally decided that with everything that I had accomplished in my life, I still was missing something. My missing link, was my Purpose!! I discovered my true Purpose at the age of fifty. We all have a Purpose in life, but we must activate it. My purpose is motivating, empowering and encouraging other women who are struggling and feeling unfulfilled in their live. Once, I decided to activate my true **purpose**, then everything started coming together for me in my life. I activated my purpose are you ready to activate yours?

Whether it's actions or behaviors, what could you STOP, do LESS of, KEEP DOING, do MORE of - and what could you START?

	STOP	Do LESS	KEEP DOING	Do MORE	START
1					
2					
3					
4					
5					

Rhonda's Story

My personal story and Luberta's parallel eerily in so many ways. I was a teen mom. By the time I was sixteen years of age I had given birth to two beautiful daughters, but by two different men. That's just how it happened.

In my family teen pregnancy was like an epidemic. My grandmothers, my mom, then me. Eventually has I got older and realized the effect on my poor decisions I decided it would be my daughters who would break the "family tradition" of teen pregnancy. I fought that battle and I won it. Though my daughters were younger than I wanted them to be, when they became mothers they were both high school graduates, living in their own homes. For those who tried to condemn my girls with negativity, God slapped them in the face. I was proud of them.

As much as this is my story and has help mold me into the woman I am today, it is what led me to my purpose. If you listened to my 2015 Change Your Mind, Change Your Life Women's International Teleconference, you'll remember that I spoke of this story: One day I was riding in the car with my mom. I remember hearing a commercial on the radio about a program or an event for teen moms. The lady on the radio said, "When you become a teen mom, your LIFE IS OVER!" She said it with such conviction, too. I remember like it was yesterday, because it bothered me so much. I remember thinking to myself at that moment it would be my mission to teach teen moms life skills and other things so they would never feel that way. I never felt that way. I just didn't feel like she had a right to make such a judgement for a teen mom, especially since I had been one.

Understand that working with teen moms is part of my purpose. It has nothing to do with money, but everything to do with a love and passion for being able to assist them any way I can. I took me a while to convince myself to do this, though. But when I finally decided to step into what God was calling me to do, He led me to an organization that houses teen moms and their children. I go there as a volunteer instructor to teach them life skills, budgeting, have panels with other women, etc. It is very liberating and I love it. I hope to do more by offering the same in high schools and colleges.

Just remember when you walk in your purpose, everything will line up just as it should.

Getting Started in Your Journey

Don't be like me and do this thing bassackwards! But I didn't know...let me explain...I began to create products and host my own events BEFORE I built my audience. All I knew when I got started was that I WAS READY! Lol. But there was no one waiting for my readiness. So, first-Get Known. But your audience. Get interviewed, collaborate with those already doing what you want to do. Volunteer, join a Meetup...the less expensive things to get started. Then Get Found. Start to market yourself...build your Brand. Begin your message. You MUST be consistent in "showing up" for your business. There are a lot of us out here; but you can still stand out. Then once you have those two mastered, now it's time to Get Paid! By now your audience is built, you have a following through your marketing and your Brand and/or message is being sought out. If you're blessed they are demanding more from you and more of you! I hope that helps.

The number one step to getting started in your journey of starting a new business or revamping the business you are currently in is to BE CLEAR.

By being CLEAR, I mean to be clear on WWWHW...WHO, WHAT, WHERE, HOW, AND WHY? The number one question you must answer before you start your business is: Does my business/service solve a problem? Your second question should be: Are people ready to PAY for the answers to that problem right now? Every day your potential customers and clients have an issue that they are trying to figure out for themselves and it's frustrating them; they are wasting time because they don't have the right resources and it's keeping them awake at night. If you have the solution to their problem and can find them, you have reached your target market. But, you need the answers to these questions even before you begin your strategic or business plan. These questions and answers set the foundation for your business model.

In the space below, I'd like you to write a summary of your business goals and how much income you'd like to generate from your business in the next 3 years. Expect to see this information change by the end of your 30 days.

Now that you have a summary of your business goals, what do you think is your life's purpose?

Applied Knowledge is Power

You have finally decided to step out on faith and start your own business. After making this decision, then you realize you don't know where or how to start this task. Well, to make this transition a little easier, here are some tips on how to get from point A to point B, regarding your new business.

1. Pray

2. Pray again, keep doing this throughout this journey

3. Decided what type of business you would like to own and even google information regarding the specific type of business that you have decided to start-up.

4. Hire a Business or Life Coach. He or she will help you understand the business aspects of being an entrepreneur. They can also give you direction and clarity on obtaining the type of lifestyle you desire to have about your business. I would also suggest hiring a Financial Coach too. The person would give you guidance on how to invest, save and variety of other financial tidbits to help you along the way about the financial part of your business.

5. Determine the name of your upcoming business and think about the people you will be selling and/or offering your products too. This is called your niche. Think about this part very carefully, even though it's not completely about the money, you still want to ensure that you can and will make a profit.

6. Decided if you want your business to be registered under the Non-Profit Organization (NPO) category or Limited Liability Cooperation (LLC). Registering and fees are different in each state, so check with an attorney prior to make the final decision.

7. Make an appointment with a professional photographer, to obtain your professional photos. Remember these photos will be used in

marketing campaigns, on your website, events, and venues where you will be selling or promoting your product and/or service. Have at least three different outfits: business, casual, and dressy. Find a good makeup artist and hair stylist. Remember these pictures reflect your business.

8. Start working on your Vision and Mission Statement for your upcoming business. The Vision Statement will address the declaration of your organization, objectives ideally based on economics foresight, intended to guide it internal decision-making. The Mission Statement will address the true purpose of the organization. Keep in mind that as your company grows and expands the above statements could change too.

9. Hire a professional website and graphic designer to assist you with building your website and logo. Review the attached checklist of additional information needed to make this task run smoother.

10. Purchase [Professional Business Cards](#).

11. If you haven't already done so, it might be a good time to become active on social media. Create business pages on Facebook, Instagram, Twitter, Periscope, Hootsuite and LinkedIn.

12. Check out these other sources for additional help and information. Small Business Administrator (SBA), Fiverr, Canva, WordPress, Aweber, and remember if all else fails, just Google what you are looking for to complete your business task.

Checklist for Website

1. Purpose and Goals

Determine what purpose your website will serve. Are you using it for selling items on line? Using it to provide information about your business? Using it mainly for blogging? After you answer those questions then it will give you a better understanding about what information you will need for your website.

2. Domain Name

This will be the name that will identify you on the internet. Choose and register your domain name. This can be done with GoDaddy.com, WordPress.com and there are several other companies, just google domain name register. Remember some are free and others require payment.

3. Priorities

Determine what is truly needed on your website to get you up and running. Remember you can always change your website, nothing is written in stone.

4. Site Pages and Features

Determine how many pages you are wanting on your website.

Required storage amount for videos and images

Tools for blogs, customer reviews, online ordering

Links or integration with social media

Shopping cart

Description of Services

Contact

Bio/About

5. Website Builder

Determine if you are going to tackle this yourself or hire a professional

6. Hosting

This will be needed so your site is available on the internet for potential customers may view from their computers. Google on line for this specific service offered.

*You will pay a fee for this particular service.

7. Connect your Domain Name to your Website

This will help potential customers find and assess your website.

8. Plan and Develop Content

This is needed to give your potential information regarding the type of service you are providing, information about you, contact information and any other pertinent information that is needed to give your potential customers a clear and specific picture regarding your business.

9. Promote your Website

Place this information on your social media outlets, business cards, advertising and online business directories.

10. Track Performance

This will help you know who have viewed your website. It will also help you to see if you need to make any changes on your website. Consider installing external analytics program with your hosting provider.

11. Continue to make updates. Remember that you can change your website.

Target Market

What does that mean? Your target market is the person or group of people who you set out to intentionally educate with your service or your business. You create them in your mind as you're one special, unique client or customer.

No two people will serve the same unique type of client in the same way. But every person that does the same business or service that you do they all have unique way of delivering information and teaching. Saying this means that there is still room for you and what it is that you bring to your special, unique client.

When you are trying to determine your target market that means that you are determining who you're talking to, what problem that they have that you can solve, where are you going to be able to find them and how can you find them.

So let's go back to the WHO. The who means specifically if you are talking to just one person, and not a whole audience, but one person what would the conversation sound like? Are you talking to a woman, a man, or young adult?

Sometimes this comes easily to people, and at other times it does not. Sometimes it takes more of you to be able to dig deeper into exactly what your own specialty is in problem-solving or the problem that you want to solve to be able to derive at who your special, unique client it's to you.

For an example, my entrepreneurship began as a real estate agent. In that market when I began, I did not have a niche market. As time went on my niche market became to be investors. That is who I worked with and for 80% of the time. That meant my property hunting and my listing were marketed for investment properties because that is what investors look for; and to make it even more simplified I sought out investment properties that took a minimum of $10,000 of repair work. Because I had such a specific niche it was easy for my business to be referred to other investors who were looking for the same type of properties.

Once you have determined your who, it is important to make them unique in your mind. So, what do they look like to you? What does your special clients look like to you? Is it a woman who is a wife or single mom?
How much does she make? Is it a man? Is he married; is he single? Is he educated? You should know these things when you are considering what your special client looks like to you so that you know how you can help them best.
Another determining factor is where do they live? These are all

indicators when you are considering your one special, unique client. The biggest thing that needs to be determined is what is the problem that they have right now today that they are willing to stop everything that they are doing in order to call you, and PAY YOU NOW to have you fix it.

Once you know what the problem is, it is essential that all of your wording in your marketing and your literature reflect that problem that you solve so that it draws that special, unique client directly to you. Knowing where your client lives in your mind determines how you will find them. We will cover more of this in your marketing chapter.

Now here is your worksheet!

it is time for you to write out who your target market is, what they look like, what they do, how much money they make where they live etc. also remember that you could have more than one target market but that means that you will need more than one marketing message. Also, if you have more than one business or service, you will have more than one target market. Copy your sheet for each target market you need to identify

My Target Market Worksheet

Male or Female _____

Age _____

Education _____

Income _____

Married/Single/Widowed/Divorced

_____

Where Do They Live? _____

Employed/Retired/Self-Employed/Students

_____

This is a great start!

When you are marketing to your target market it is important to note that not every type of person will be attracted to every type of marketing message. this means you have a different marketing message each type of customer you are trying to reach within your target market. For example, women entrepreneurs; single moms; and married women are just an example of different groups who may receive different types of marketing messaging or wording differently. The same type of marketing message will not attract them to you because they are in totally different groups within your market.

G. A. I. N

Get in position- Where are you now? Take a good look at the room you're sitting in. Is it cluttered? Junky? In need of cleaning? Disorganized? The room you spend the most amount of time in looks a lot like your life right now. If it needs decluttering, it is probably because you are out of position. Your story, your success, your book, your invention, your intellectual property has someone on the other end waiting for you to get into position. If you are out of position, they cannot get into position. Do you believe that? God can't show up for you to do what He needs to do if you're not in the correct position to receive it. So, if he told you to move and you didn't move then you're missing your blessings that were depended on THAT move. So, let's get into position. How do you get into position?

1)   By accepting responsibility for your inactions. Get rid of your excuses and start a plan of action

2)   Look at your circle of influence

3)   Get off social media and get face to face

4)   Concentrate on your niche', craft, product (not your website)

5)   Act on your Why. Stop giving up on God's plan for you when the bottom falls out. Don't quit on your marriage because your husband isn't being husbandly...Don't leave your job because you don't like your supervisor. Stop making your life look a patch quilt because you won't stay in position!

*God wants to prosper you
*Your Gifts are given specifically to you. You are FEARFULLY and WONDERFULLY made.
*Philippians
Put a DEMAND ON YOUR POTENTIAL

Assess Your Risk Factor - As a business owner or entrepreneur or even as a person it is up to you to develop and understand your risk factor.

Some of us are willing to take huge risks to reap substantial gains. Meaning investing a lot of money, time, and resources to get what they want out of their business or personal lives.

Others of us are only able to handle bits at a time because our risk level is low. This could be for two reasons:

Your MINDSET is not where it should be to grow your business or make changes in your life OR

You are simply not equipped to be a full-time entrepreneur/business owner or maybe should not take on whatever is going on in your personal life now (which is perfectly fine)

Invest in yourself- I just need to share what 2 things I learned from investing in myself. The first one is the ROI. Return on investment is greater than my initial investment. You must come to realize that when you pay money to grow your business you are investing in information or enhancing your skillset. This can be used over and over for years to come. Not only that you could possibly can another marketable skill for yourself which means you have yet another trade that someone is willing to pay you to teach them to do NOW. Secondly, is it's the proof. Believe me when you invest in yourself it shows. It's shows in your growth. It shows in your circle of influence and it shows in your words. If you are not evolving, neither is your business.

Decide how much you are going to invest in your business monthly then commit to doing that. If you are just beginning and can only invest in your business sporadically for now, don't be ashamed of that, but make it count. If this is you and you receive an income tax refund, then at the beginning of each year you should already have planned how many conferences or courses you plan to attend during the year. When you get your large lump sum of money, you need to be investing in those IN FULL right away. That way when they come around they are already paid for and you are set to go. If you are making money in your business monthly or if you are still bringing in income from employment or other resources you should be making a conscious effort to hire a coach of join a program.

Never give up- Let's say your favorite cake was a pineapple upside down cake. One day you decide to make it. The first time it didn't quite turn out as you hoped. Would you try to make it again? Of course, you would. This time you'd be extra careful about the ingredients and how long you put it in the oven and make sure it's one the right temperature, right? The same thing goes for your business. There may be several recipes to get to the same cake just as there may be more than one road that leads to the success or growth of your business. You just need to find the right path for you.

If you are at a point right now where you feel stuck and you cannot afford a coach, I want you to do these things. Scrap all the things that you know aren't working. The definition of insanity is to do the same things over and over expecting the same results. STOP IT. You need to revamp.

1)   Go back and look over your notes. What did you skip or leave out? Did you take any short cuts?

2)   Call back or follow up with anyone on your list that you have not talked to in a while. This includes anyone who may have responded positively to a Facebook post or Tweet or sent you an inbox message.

3)   Have you sent out an email marketing campaign lately? If you haven't your subscribers may not know what you are up to or know the latest product you have available. Everyone cannot possibly see everything that is posted in social media.

4)   Get out and network

5)   Join local events by vending or becoming a sponsor.

"I can do all things through Christ which strengthened me."

Whether we achieve our goals depends on whether we take action. But what decides whether we take action in the first place? How motivated you are! So, simply **pick your Top 3 goals**, then **answer the questions below**. Keep writing even if you repeat your answers. The information below will help you feel clear, focused and more motivated to achieve your goals.

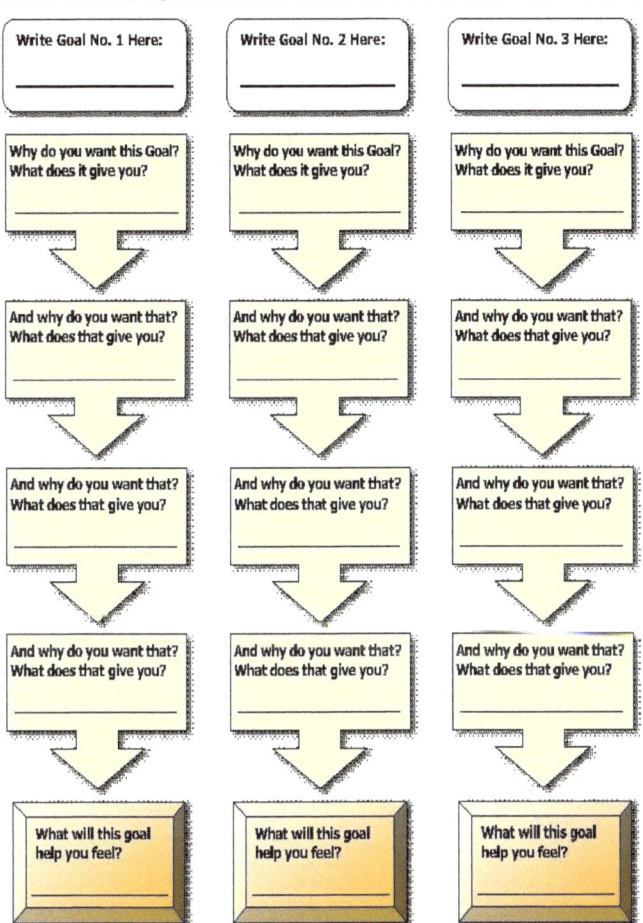

Write Goal No. 1 Here:	Write Goal No. 2 Here:	Write Goal No. 3 Here:

Why do you want this Goal? What does it give you?

And why do you want that? What does that give you?

And why do you want that? What does that give you?

And why do you want that? What does that give you?

What will this goal help you feel?

The Balancing Act: How Bad Do You Want It?
Luberta's Journey

Become an entrepreneur is something, that will truly take you out of your comfort zone, because it will make you feel uncomfortable. That uncomfortable feeling is called growth. This feeling has good and bad parts to it. The good is, why do you want to become stagnant in life? The bad is, I just don't like moving out of my comfort zone. To accomplish anything worth having, you must endure stepping out of your comfort zone.

My decision to start own business came after discussing this with my significant other. He was cool with it in the beginning, but then he noticed that wife spent a lot of time on conference call, being on the computer, attending variety of meetings. He didn't like the fact that our relationship had been placed on the back burner. In addition to starting this business, I still had my 9 to 5 job. This meant that I can only work on my business, during my off hours and days off from work. Did this pose a problem for our relationship? Yes, it did, but we finally had to talk to determine what we could do. Starting this business is very important to me, but keeping my marriage on track is too. I must make sacrificing in both areas. I am learning how to manage my time better, to ensure that both areas in my life a receiving equally amounts of attention. I am very passionate about my new career choice. I will succeed in both areas. It's called time managing. I know that my desire to obtain this goal is going to outweigh my desire of being concerned about stepping out of my comfort zone. I have stayed up several nights working on projects knowing that I should be in bed due to having to work the next day, but for me to accomplish my goal and desire to help other people, I must be willing to make those sacrifices. I have gone to work on just a few hours of sleep, but my adrenaline kicks in and makes me feel like I have slept for hours. If you want something to change in your life you must be willing to make those changes too. My desire to accomplish this goal is currently outweighing my desire to just return to my so-called normal life.

If you had decided that you want something new in your life are you willing to step out of your comfort zone and accomplish your goals? Are you willing to make sacrifices to ensure that your personally life doesn't interfere with your business life? Can it be done, yes, but you must be willing to make those hard choices and decision during this transitional phase in your life. Determine why you want this new chapter in your life. Make the decision and explain to your family, and friends that this is something that you want and will accomplish, but they must also be willing to work with you during this time.

Once, you make the decision to make changes in your current life, then you will find it very hard to return. If you don't like something in your life, then change it and if you are not willing to make the changes then quit complaining about your life. So, the question remains, how bad do you want this and what are you willing to do to accomplish your goal? It's not that hard or complicated to figure out, you just need to be willing to balance out the two. You can have the best of both worlds, if you work at it.

Rhonda's Journey

When you become an entrepreneur whether you are starting out new or if you have been quite some time you were married that it is definitely a balancing act. It is a balance between your business, your family, having time for yourself, and if you were still working that 9-to-5 job that as well.

My first entrepreneurship opportunity came to me when I was in real estate. In the beginning, I was still working my 9-to-5 job and I thought I could build up enough clientele to go full-time as a real estate agent. Let me tell you I was in for some very late nights and some early-mornings! Because I was still working Monday through Friday from 8 AM until 4 PM the only time I had to work in my real estate business was on the weekend or in the evening times. But because I was a single mom my evenings to work on my business didn't start until after I'd get my son to bed. So, that meant I was up many nights well past 2 AM going over listings. putting information together, going through the MLS, returning emails, trying to discover new neighborhoods that I wanted to call home, going through the newspaper-whatever it was that I need to do I was doing it during that time, so come Saturday morning I'd have all the information I needed and I was ready to go! You know what? I don't even remember being tired during that time although I know I had to be, right? But I wanted success so badly in real estate and I carried that passion, because I was in love with my career choice, I was willing to do whatever I needed.

What I will tell you is that if you are doing it for the money your will power and your stamina will die out. If you have a passion for whatever it is that you do, and you really love it, you will last a lot longer and the money will come more naturally. Don't just pick a business because it can make you money. Lots of entrepreneurs or business owners make this mistake then later you see them failing because it wasn't what they wanted in the beginning. So now I ask you: how bad do you want it?

NetWorthing

I like to call networking NetWorthing. Why? Because it outlines in action. When you were simply networking a lot of people are exchanging information or business cards but on forgetting to go back to that person to exchange I Do's to find out how you can benefit one another. Typically, when I go to a networking event I usually do not carry business cards. For me it became more daunting than it was fun to network. I ended up with more business cards then I knew what to do with! Now with smart phones are use my iPhone and input that person's information directly into my phone with their name, company's name, and I can assign them to a group so I know which networking event I met them. It makes it easier for me to go back to the contact when I need to know what type of person I want to work with for a certain project. As most of us know the money is always in the follow up So, if you meet a great person whom you can benefit both ways and you failed to do the follow up with them by reaching back out to them, setting a meeting, collaborating with them then you could have missed a grand opportunity. Therefore, instead of calling it networking, I call it NetWorthing!

In order to make networthing less stressful, practice your 1-minute conversation, also referred to as your pitch, as well as your 3-minute conversation. For example, my 1 minute conversation goes like this: "I coach women to reposition their money #mindsets to build systems and leverage multiple streams of income from their business through private coaching, & more."

Affirmations

A very important aspect in the beginning as well as throughout your business is POSITIVE THINKING. Your mindset will be the common factor of accountability to your success or failure along with finance, money management, and marketing.

Affirmations are detailed sentences written by you that are positive, and that will keep you headed in the direction you should be. These should be kept in a visible location, such as your bathroom mirror, and be spoken OUT LOUD every day, at least once a day.

Here's an example: I am no longer a 9-5 employee. I am an income earning entrepreneur earning over $5000 a month from various sources.

Now it's time for you to take a moment and write 10 Affirmations. Remember to be positive and detailed. Your affirmations can be related to business, family, success, health, etc.

Do You Have Tenacity?

So why is it that we are fearful of ourselves? Could it be that we are so fearful of the success that we may achieve? I want you to remember that fear is never in your present. It is about your past or your future. The past because of a prior bad experience or mistake that prevents you from taking a chance again for fear of the same result. The future, because simply put many of us fear the unknown.

It is true when they say that in order to continue to grow your mindset you must surround yourself with like-minded people or even better surround yourself with people who know much more than you do. Do not be caught up in the whirlwind of believing that you are not worthy of your own success. Your success story will not be like someone else's so there's no need to try to mimic someone else's success journey you will have your own. Once you stop believing what other people believe about you and start growing yourself and start introducing yourself to new mindsets, new strategies, new networking partnerships then you will in able to start understanding that you are worth the success that she was driving for. In business, there will be many ups and downs. Success does not look fancy. It can be a rugged road, but you must stay your course. Don't allow your pauses to become permanent STOPS. All your experiences will build your resistance to change and your tenacity will become stronger and stronger!

Meet the Authors
Luberta

I live in a small town called Centralia, IL. My past truly didn't determine my future. Most people in my little town considered me just another teenage mother, who would remain on welfare instead of doing something with her life.

Being a success story is something almost unheard from someone residing in this small town. I consider myself a small-town girl with big city dreams. I truly believe if you change your mindset, it will change your life.

I am currently involved in another book collaboration called Millionaire Mom and my chapter is called Drive and Determination. This book center around me being a teenage mother and becoming a success story. I am also writing my autobiography called Heal the Hurt and it will be released in December of 2016.

I am truly thankful for all of the blessing and obstacles that have I have endured in my fifty years of living, because they have helped me become the woman that I am at this moment.

B.U.I.L.D

Brand your message

Uphold Your Integrity

Involve Others

Leave Naysayers Behind

Deliver Greatness

Special Video for E-books Only.

Its Miss Rhonda!

I come from a small town in St. Louis, Missouri called Kinloch. People don't think you can be a success coming out of a neighborhood that once meant so much to the community historically; that has now been riddled to destruction, and add to that being a teen mom.

I went from having the mentality of being that welfare chick to an entrepreneurial mindset. If I can do it, anyone can do it. It's not easy. It takes work and TENACITY (latest chapter in book collaboration with Stevii Aisha Mills: Cultivating Your IT Factor).

Success is defined by different people in different ways. In my terms, I am successful at everything I do, because I tried. If you don't ever try, you will never know.

I can contribute my success to a run as a Realtor, which is how I learned about entrepreneurship; to know being a successful author, speaker, mentor, and business startup coach.

I know you will enjoy my books whether you are reading my fiction writings or one of my books written to make you successful in your business!

Bonus Material

GREAT Goals are:

a) **Outcome focused**: Once you understand your WHY (and it's an enthusiastic WHY) you're 90% there!

b) **In line with your values:** The more a goal aligns with your inner or core values - the EASIER it will be to achieve. NOTE: We can achieve goals that don't align with our values but it's harder to do and less satisfying.

c) **Stated in the positive:** i.e. "I want healthy fingernails" rather than "I want to stop biting my nails"

and SMART:

Specific (so you know exactly what you're trying to achieve)

Measurable (so you know when you've achieved it!)

Action-oriented (so you can DO something about it!)

Realistic (so it IS achievable) and

Time-Bound (has a deadline)

Focusing on the Outcome:

1. What is it that you really, REALLY want? *Dig deep...*
2. What is the SPECIFIC outcome you're looking for?
3. What is the PAIN for you of NOT achieving your goal?

Aligning with your Values:

4. Is this goal in line with your life vision/overall life-plan? *(Don't know - what does your gut tell you?)*
5. Is this goal in line with your values? *(Unsure? Ask yourself what's REALLY important to you in life - will this goal help you achieve more of that?)*
6. Are the goals something YOU truly want, or are they something you think you SHOULD have or SHOULD be doing? *(Tip: If it is a SHOULD, it may be someone else's dream...)*
7. When you think about your goal does it give you a sense of deep contentment or 'rightness', happiness and/or excitement? *(If so, these are good signs that it's a healthy goal.)*

8. If you could have the goal RIGHT NOW – would you take it? *(If not, why not? What issues are there?)*
9. How does this goal fit into your life/lifestyle? *(Time/effort/commitments/who else might be impacted?)*

Identifying Obstacles:

10. Can YOU start & maintain this goal/outcome? *(i.e. Do you have complete control over achieving it?)*
11. How will making this change affect other aspects of your life? *(i.e. What else might you need to deal with?)*
12. What's good about your CURRENT SITUATION? *(i.e. What's the benefit of staying right where you are?)* Then ask, how can I keep those good aspects while STILL making this change?
13. WHAT might you have to give up/stop doing to achieve this goal? *(Essentially, what's the price of making this change – and are you willing to pay it?)*
14. If there was something important around achieving this goal (to help you succeed, or that could get in the way) that you haven't mentioned yet, what would it be?
15. WHO will you have to BE to achieve this goal?

Goal Sizing:

16. Is your goal the right size to be working on? *Too big? Break down into smaller goals. Too small? Fit into a larger goal.*
17. What would be the MINIMUM/Super-Easy level of goal to achieve?
18. What would be your TARGET level of goal to achieve?
19. What would be your EXTRAORDINARY level of goal to achieve?

Resources - get moving:

20. What RESOURCES do you already have to help you achieve your goal? Make a list! *(e.g. things, support from people, contacts, personal qualities, knowledge, skills, money, time etc.).*
21. What RESOURCES do you NEED to help you achieve your goal? Make a list!

IMPORTANT: REMEMBER – GOALS are there to INSPIRE YOU not to beat yourself up with!

www.ingramcontent.com/pod-product-compliance
Lightning Source LLC
Chambersburg PA
CBHW040925180526
45159CB00002BA/618